Be Unique and Memorable .... pg. 3

Everyone's Favorite Topic .... pg. 4

Starting Conversations .... pg. 5

How to Get a Better Response .... pg. 8

Stop Stopping Conversations! .... pg. 9

Success is in the Details .... pg. 13

Four Elevator Pitch Mistakes .... pg. 14

    But I Do So Much More .... pg. 14

    New Crowd, New Elevator Pitch .... pg. 17

    Leaving Empty Handed Means Failure ....pg. 20

    I've Always Done It This Way .... pg. 22

The Conversational Elevator Pitch .... pg. 23

    How's it going? .... pg. 25

    What do you do? .... pg. 29

    How do you do that? .... pg. 33

The 30-Second Elevator Pitch .... pg. 36

    Grab their Attention .... pg. 38

    Begin the Conversation .... pg. 41

    Call them to Action .... pg. 45

Examples of a 30-Second Elevator Pitch .... pg. 48

And One More Thing .... pg. 50

Appendix A:

    Answering What do you Do Worksheet .... pg. 52

Appendix B:

    30-Second Elevator Pitch Worksheet .... pg. 54

Michele –
Start great
conversations!

Andy

You are already unique and memorable.

You are!

You just haven't learned to express your passion and commitment in a way that inspires people to call you.

If you've ever struggled to explain what makes you different…

If your message isn't getting across the way you want it to…

This is the perfect book for you!

My name is Andrew Winig, and I spent years watching people's eyes glaze over as I tried to explain what I do.

Through trial and error, over many years, and quite by accident, I finally stumbled onto the secret of the 30-Second Elevator Pitch.

Now my Elevator Pitch starts great Business Conversations.

Every time.

I am eager to share this knowledge with you because you have a great service and an incredible depth of expertise.

Now it's time to tell the world in a way that makes them want to spread the word.

It's time to grab people's attention. Let's get started…

The Elevator Pitch is a series of techniques for starting conversations.

So why are most people so reluctant to give their Elevator Pitch?

Simple. Because most people think that they have to do all the talking.

Big Mistake!

Why?

Because you can't start a conversation if you're doing all the talking.

Wait! How can you get the other person talking during your Elevator Pitch?

Aha! That is the million dollar question.

And as you'll discover shortly,

The answer is much, much simpler than you've been led to believe.

To understand why, we need to start with...

> {
> An effective elevator pitch
> starts business conversations
> that lead to leads.
> }

What is the purpose of the Elevator Pitch?

To start a conversation.

That's it.

And the absolutely worst ways to start conversations are to

> √ Try to prove your expertise
> √ Show off your skills and talents
> √ List everything you could possibly do for someone.

Because that's all about you.

And other people want to talk about themselves.

So the key to an effective Elevator Pitch is to say something, then wait for the other person to respond.

Once they respond, you are in a conversation!

And it's a relief to learn that business networking gets much, much easier, more relaxing, and even more rewarding when you don't have to carry the whole conversation by yourself.

By the way, the surest sign that you need a better Elevator Pitch is if someone says:

"That's interesting"

Why?

Because "That's interesting" is a conversation stopper.

Instead, you want them to say something like:

> √ "How do you do that?"
> √ "Tell me more about that"
> √ "Could you also handle a situation where...?"

That keeps the conversation moving forward.

Here's how to get people to respond in a way that starts conversations...

If you don't like the way people respond to your Elevator Pitch, change what you're saying until you get a response that's closer to what you want.

How do people respond to your Elevator Pitch?

Maybe you know someone like my client.

Before she worked with me,

If you had asked her what she did,

She would say she was a mortgage broker.

And at the time, according to the newspapers, the real estate market was struggling.

So people would respond: "Oh, I'm so sorry to hear that. It must be a terrible time for you."

The truth was that she was doing quite well,

Except that her elevator pitch was putting her on the defensive so fast that she could not convince people that great mortgages were actually available.

So she made a simple change.

Now she talks about the details...

Most elevator pitches are way too vague.

"I'm a mortgage broker" doesn't work.

Because that person doesn't think they need a mortgage broker right now.

So the conversation stops.

And you don't connect.

But wait!

The fact that they don't think they need a mortgage broker

Doesn't mean that they don't need your services!

Because (and I hate to be the one to break this to you):

Bonus Elevator Pitch Tip!

Your goal is to show how you are different from everyone else. Yet if you describe what you do by your title or your profession, then you sound just like everyone else who does that work!

No one is actually looking for a mortgage broker.

- √ They want to buy a home
  (except they think that they can't get the money)
- √ They have considered refinancing their home
  (but are afraid of closing costs)
- √ They need cash for a project
  (and hadn't considered the equity in their home)

Note that this is true for any profession.

No one thinks they need a lawyer, but

- √ One of their employees just made accusations against another employee
- √ They're getting ready to roll out a new employee benefit
- √ Her friend just got served with divorce papers.

Want a few more?

No one thinks they need an IT professional, but

- √ His daughter can't get a strong wireless signal in her attic bedroom
- √ Her son can't get access to the kitchen printer from the basement computer
- √ They're pretty sure they're running nightly backups of their key systems...

No one thinks they need a landscape architect, but

- √ They're embarrassed to entertain friends in their back yard
- √ They avoid looking at their front yard when they drive into their driveway
- √ They know that tree is dead. They just aren't sure what to do about it

So how do we fix this?

We provide details...

Back to our mortgage broker.

Here's what she says now when people ask what she does:

"As an example, I recently helped a young couple purchase their very first home"

Now people ask her a flurry of questions

> √ "People are actually buying houses right now?"
> √ "Funny you should say that. My son wants to buy a house but assumed that he and his wife couldn't get financing."
> √ "You know, my wife and I are thinking about refinancing our home. Could you help us with that?"

Did you notice what just happened?

These people just volunteered all sorts of information about themselves.

Information that makes it easier to have a meaningful conversation with them.

For example:

> √ "Of course people are buying. Were you considering selling?"
> √ "I have a great program for first time homebuyers that makes houses much more affordable. Would you be interested in hearing more about it?

√ "Of course I can help with a refinancing
   When would be a good time to sit down with
   you and your wife so I can hear what you
   have in mind?"

At this moment, the Elevator Pitch has led you naturally and conversationally into a sales conversation.

But beware...

My mortgage broker client quickly protests:

"But I don't just work with first time homebuyers. I do refis and cash-outs. I help with relocation and empty nesters. I don't want to limit myself."

I told her what I'll tell you:

Remember that the Purpose of the Elevator Pitch

It is not to show off your expertise.

It is not to give a laundry list of your products.

It is to START a business conversation.

Once you are sitting in front of legitimate prospect...

Then you can demonstrate your expertise.

Then you can explore other ways you can help them.

Then you can share your process for getting results.

The Elevator Pitch starts conversations.

And you can't start a conversation about everything.

So you have to pick one thing to start the conversation.

How do you pick which one?

I worked with an insurance agent who had two great client success stories.

The first was about insuring art for a traveling art show.

The second was how she discovered that a restaurant owner didn't have liquor liability coverage for one of his restaurants that served alcohol.

People outside the art world aren't that concerned with insuring art.

Yet everyone has concerns about alcohol, drinking, and drunk driving.

As you can imagine, she consistently gets a better response to the second story.

You want a topic that ties into something people are already talking about.

Bonus Elevator Pitch Tip!

The best Elevator Pitch will only start conversations about 15% of the time. That's right! Everyone is always surprised to hear that most of the time, even the best Elevator Pitch will not start a conversation. That's OK. Shake that person's hand, say it was nice to meet them, and that you're going to go continue networking. In a room of 30 people, if you start conversations with 3 or 4 of them, that's a great night of networking.

I have been using exactly the same Elevator Pitch now for over 5 years.

And the most amazing thing starts to happen.

People remember me.

Every time they see me,

In any context,

They hear the same message.

They know who I am.

They know what I offer.

They trust me and my message.

That can't happen if you're always coming up with something new to say.

And when you combine saying the same thing every time with using specific details, that's when you'll start getting better results.

Do you think you'll get more leads as a lawyer, or as the person who "helps people test drive their homes before they buy them."

Do you think more people will approach you as a family entertainer, or as the person who "offers Star Wars Jedi Training birthday parties for 10 year old boys"

Now, are these statements limiting?

No!

In fact, it's the opposite.

Why would you want to test drive a new home? The lawyer can talk about the work he does protecting people from bad contracts, which engages people who may not have known that they needed a lawyer.

The family entertainer was concerned about focusing on boys. What he found actually happens is that parents approach him and ask "So what's your signature event for girls?"

Details engage your prospects.

Bonus Elevator Pitch Tip!

People are eager to change their Elevator Pitch when they're not happy with the results. Once you have an Elevator Pitch that consistently starts the right kind of conversations with the right kind of people, you won't ever want to change it!

Your Elevator Pitch does not close sales.

It starts conversations that lead to sales.

You have to get used to knowing that an event was worthwhile, even and especially when you're leaving empty handed.

Here's an example of an Elevator Pitch that led to a big sale years later:

A business litigation attorney who I had known for years once made an offhand comment about one of her clients: "I wish he had called me first."

She had litigated, for this employer, a very nasty employee situation that could have been headed off entirely if the employer had taken certain steps before rolling out a particular benefits package.

This lawyer is always willing to litigate, but she prefers to help her clients avoid being sued.

Years later...

Yes, at least 3 years later I was facing a sticky employee situation in my business. And her words echoed through my head "I wish he had called me first."

So I picked up the phone and called. In just a few hours she protected me, my other employees, and my business from a very dangerous rogue employee. I happily wrote her a check for keeping me out of years of litigation.

See, the real power of the elevator pitch is in planting the seeds for future conversations. Normally I wouldn't have recognized that moment as a good time to call my lawyer. Yet that offhand comment by my lawyer saved me tens of thousands of dollars.

My lawyer didn't get any results that day she mentioned her client. The results came later. Because she planted the seeds.

She taught me to call her when the time was right for me.

It can be uncomfortable to stand out in the crowd.

It takes courage to use a different style Elevator Pitch than everyone who stood up before you.

I'll guarantee you, though, that discomfort fades rapidly when people start running up to you with leads.

Once I decided to, it still took me several months to stop starting my Elevator Pitch with "Hi, my name is Andy." It was safe and comfortable to begin that way. It had become a habit. A habit that does not work nearly as well as the techniques I outline in this book.

Here's your action step: Pick a detail and use it for the next two weeks. A detail that is uncomfortably specific. It feels dangerous, and it works.

Once you experience how details start better business conversations, you'll use them every time.

So far we've been talking about using specifics to start conversations.

And it turns out that there are only three conversations you'll ever be asked to start.

And your 30-Second Elevator Pitch starts... none of them!

Here's why.

As we've said, the Elevator Pitch is about starting a conversation.

The 30-Second Elevator Pitch is designed to start conversations when you introduce yourself to a room full of people.

You know the kind of situation I mean.

You go around the table and each person stands up for 30-40 seconds to introduce themselves to everyone else.

In the next section we'll show you step-by-step how to develop your own personalized 30-Second Elevator Pitch.

But that's not the biggest opportunity at most networking events.

Because most of the time, you're not introducing yourself to a room full of people.

Most of the time, someone walks up to you, shakes your hand, and asks you one of three questions.

And as you know, responding to any sort of face-to-face question with any sort of rehearsed speech is, well, awkward.

So here, now, is how to answer the only three questions you'll ever be asked:

√ "How's it going?"
√ "What do you do?"
√ "How do you do that?"

Let's start with "How's it going?"

I call this question the biggest missed opportunity in all of sales.

Because this technique alone will give you five more conversations a day.

And before you panic, I'm not suggesting that you knock on a few more doors or make a bunch more phone dials.

Nope. This opportunity is much more powerful than that and already exists in your daily routine.

And most people walk right past it.

What does it look like?

Someone comes up to you. A friend, an acquaintance, a stranger, an enemy, and says:

"How's it going?"

How do most people respond?

"Fine." "Same old same old." "Just trying to get by."

The Biggest Missed Opportunity in all of Sales!

From now on, any time you're asked "How's it going?", just share an example of something that is going extremely well.

Here's the template:

Awesome! I just <something awesome you just did>."

Here's our first example:

"Awesome! I just shared a powerful technique for starting better conversations."

Now, the first reaction most people have to this example is:

"Really, Andy? Awesome? What, did you grow up in the 80's or something?"

Well, yes. As a matter of fact, I did grow up in the 80's.

Awesome works for me, and it may not be your style.

And that's fine.

If you don't like awesome, use great, fantastic, incredible, better than ever, fair to middlin'.

Any positive upbeat superlative.

Let's look at another example:

"Fantastic: I just hit the game winning home run for my softball team."

Now, why would one use a personal story in a business context?

Well, I'll be the first to tell you that some personal stories have no business in any sort of business situation.

Remember, though, that the goal is to start a conversation.

And you do that by finding common ground.

And if the person in front of you also plays softball,

Or just got back from vacation in Disney World,

Or also loves planting hydrangeas,

Now you have something to talk about.

And conversations started on shared interests are the most likely to lead to a connection and further conversations.

Here's another example:

"Amazing! I just helped a young couple purchase their very first home."

You may recognize this as our mortgage broker friend.

And remember that her concern was: "Doesn't this limit me?"

But it doesn't.

It's exactly the opposite.

Because when she's this specific, people ask self-qualifying questions.

"Do you also handle refis" ("Why sure, do you know someone who's looking to refinance?")

"Do you work with baby boomers" ("Of course. Is this person looking to buy or sell?")

Or maybe, just maybe, they won't say anything.

Which is perfectly OK.

You won't start a conversation with everyone.

Just reach out, shake their hand, tell them that it was nice meeting them and that you're going to continue networking.

Then go start a conversation with someone else.

Specifics start the right kinds of conversations.

With the right people.

So, pull out the worksheet at the end of this book and come up with a few "How's it going" responses that are specific to you.

Got 'em?

Great. Let's continue...

It's the most dreaded question in all of business networking:

"What do you do?"

And this one's easy.

As long as you avoid the temptation to try to cram your years of expertise into a 30 second sound bite.

You want 7 to 10 words that get them to respond.

I'll say that again.

You want to say 7 to 10 words that get them to respond.

Remember that the goal is to start a conversation.

Once they respond, you're in a conversation!

Much more natural.

Much more engaging.

Here's the template

"I help <a group of people> <take an action>."

Here's an example from one of my clients:

"I help mothers empower their teenagers."

Note that we are still being super specific.

Specifics start conversations.

This client gets questions like:

"Oh, could you work with my mother?"

"Do you ever work with men?"

"I want to empower my employees. Does that count?"

Note that each of these responses pre-qualifies the person she's talking to.

Now she knows what interests them!

That makes for a much more productive conversation.

When you use details, people respond.

That's starting conversations!

Here's an example for a leadership trainer:

"I help employers select, hire and manage the right employees for the right jobs."

Like the business lawyer I talked about earlier, this statement helps people know when to call this leadership trainer.

When they're getting ready to hire.

When they're facing a management challenge.

So, "What do you do?"

You help a <group of people> <take an action>.

Go for a very specific group of people and a very specific action.

"I help a man in a second marriage make sure his property passes down to his kids from his first marriage."

"I work with software developers who are burnt out from working in Corporate America."

"I provide CPR training for doctors offices and nursing homes."

Pull out the worksheet at the end of this book and write down your "I help <a group of people> <take an action>."

Great work!

Remember, that the goal is to start a conversation.

So tell them what you do (in 7 to 10 words),

Then wait for a response.

Bonus Elevator Pitch Tip!

If someone doesn't respond, a great non-awkward way to restart the conversation is to ask "So, do you come to a lot of these kinds of events?"

We've looked at two of the three questions: "How's it going?" and "What do you do?"

Now let's look at "How do you do that?"

This is the bridge between the Conversational and the 30-Second Elevator Pitch.

The client success story.

The mistake most people make is that they share this information too soon.

The person you're talking to has to be interested in this information before you share it.

How do you know when they're interested.

I'll take you step-by-step through the process right now:

"How's it going?"

"Awesome. A client just landed a big contract through business networking."

"Really? What is it that you do?"

"I help solo professionals improve their Elevator Pitch."

"How do you do that?"

...

See how that works?

Now you're in a productive conversation.
And now they've expressed genuine interest in what you do.
So here's your chance to really talk about what you
enjoy talking about.

You can talk about the great work you do for your
clients.

So think about a recent client success.

Got one?

Now pull out the worksheet and put it in the following
format:

"A <business> approached me through <a referral> for
<a reason>.

If I were doing this for my business:

"A business lawyer approached me at a networking
event because cold calling wasn't working to grow his
practice."

Then:

"We rolled out <a project> which addressed <their
challenge> so now they get <a benefit>."

Again, in my case:

A mere two months after joining my Trusted Advisor Community, he is excited and confident about his Elevator Pitch, and generates enough opportunities from the networking he was already doing that he no longer needs to do any cold calling.

Here's what my mortgage broker client says:

"I was working with a young couple who was pretty sure they weren't going to be able to afford a new home in the town they wanted. After going through my comprehensive process we found several homes and qualified them for a first time buyer discount that made the home much more affordable than they expected. I'm happy to report that they moved in last month."

Pull out the worksheet at the back of this book and come up with your own.

Now you're ready to start conversations no matter what question you're asked.

And, now you're ready to work on your 30-Second Elevator Pitch...

Over the next few pages, you're going to learn the three elements of an effective 30-Second Elevator Pitch.

I'm going to help you craft your own personalized power question, client success story, and call to action.

Then I'll show you how to combine those into an effective 30-Second Elevator Pitch that inspires people to run up to you with leads.

I like to refer to these three elements as the ABC's.

Remember, that the purpose of a 30-Second Elevator Pitch is to start conversations when you stand up and introduce yourself to a room full of people.

And in that moment, when you stand up, look around, and open your mouth to speak, it doesn't matter what message you provide if people aren't ready to hear it.

Most of the time, most people have already tuned out.

So you have to grab their Attention.

'A' stands for Attention.

In a minute you'll develop a Power Question that grabs their attention because you're making it about them.

Then, once you have their attention, you have to deliver the message.

The right message.

The message that Begins the conversation.

'B' stands for Begin the conversation.

In just a few minutes you'll see that you already know the answer that instantly differentiates you from any current or future competitor.

We'll show you how to use that answer to start conversations in a room full of people.

Then, 'C' stands for Call to action.

You want your message to travel to the far corners of your business network, inspiring the right people to call you at the right time for them with the perfect opportunities for you.

Shortly, you'll develop a call to action that has people eager to jump up and give you their contact information.

Grab their Attention
Begin the conversation
Call them to action.

Let's start with grab their Attention.

We human beings love a good story.

So when you tell someone that you're going to tell them a story.

They lean in.

Ready to hear it.

And that's all you need.

Now you have their attention.

So a simple and very strong way to start your Elevator Pitch is:

"I do a lot of things, so today I'm going to share a quick example of a recent client success..."

This is the fastest way to improve your Elevator Pitch. Instead of starting with your name, title, and company name, tell them that you're going to tell them a story.

Ready for an even more advanced technique?

When you use a customized power question, you let them know how the story you're telling directly relates to them.

So how do you customize a power question?

Here are a few examples to get you started:

"When was the last time you printed and saved a thank you email?"

This gets people thinking about how much of an impression other people make when they thank them, and gets them ready to hear about this business coach's novel approach to sending a customized, physical thank you.

Here's another example:

"Everyone knows that getting a speeding ticket increases your car insurance rates. You may be doing things that increase your health insurance rates."

What are you doing that increases your health insurance rates? This insurance agent will be happy to send you his white paper and talk to you about ways to reduce your health insurance costs.

Here's another one:

"I work with people who are renovating their bathroom."

This is so powerful because it's easy to self-select into this group.

People either have plans to renovate their bathroom, or they don't.

So they instantly know whether they (or their friends) should be talking to this glass artist.

So those are the three templates for a power question:

"When was the last time _____?"

"Everyone knows that
_____.You may be doing
something that _____."

"I work with people who are
_____."

Pull out the worksheet at the end of this book, pick a template, and fill in your own power question.

Good! Now it's time to Begin the Conversation.

Remember the story about my business lawyer?

She said "I wish my client had called me before he rolled out that employee policy."

Her client could have saved hundreds of thousands of dollars and years of litigation.

That's why you use a client success story.

A specific success story.

About a specific client.

The details give people something to hold on to.

Something to connect to.

And a reason to call you in the future.

Remember that the more you generalize, the more you sound like everyone else.

The more you use specific details, the more you differentiate yourself.

Here's what I mean:

Everyone provides outstanding service to their customers.

That's not a differentiator.

So instead of saying that you provide outstanding customer service, talk about a particular time you (or your employees) went the extra mile for a customer.

"A customer emailed me on a Tuesday to prepare for an Elevator Pitch Contest on Thursday. We scheduled a last-minute Elevator Pitch Complete Coaching Session and her new Elevator Pitch went on to win the competition."

People will want that kind of service for themselves, so they'll call you.

Here's another example:

Everyone believes that they offer the best product.

That's not a differentiator.

So instead of saying that you offer the best product

Talk about a particular time that your product or service delighted your customer.

"A business coaching client used the Elevator Pitch he developed in our Elevator Pitch Complete Coaching Session at a networking event 2 days later, and two people approached him to do presentations for their companies."

People want to be delighted the same way, so they'll call you.

OK, ready to do this for your business?

Pull out the worksheet at the end of this book,

Think about a particular customer you work with who is a perfect customer.

They face exactly the right problem.

You have exactly the right solution.

And they are delighted with your work.

Now, in the context of that specific customer, answer the following six questions rapidly, just write down the first few words that come to mind for each question.

Ready, here we go:

How did this customer find you?

_____

Why were they looking for you?

_____

What business are they in?

_____

What were (are) their challenges?

_____

How do you help them?

_____

What benefits do they see?

_____

Great!

Now use those answers to fill in the client success template:

Client Success

I was approached by a _____ who
{type of business}
was facing _____.
{business challenge}
We rolled out our _____ and
{product or service}
now they _____.
{benefit}

You're almost there!

You've grabbed their attention, and begun the conversation.

Now let's call them to action...

My franchised window cleaning business succeeds on an interesting premise.

On any given day, in any given town, on any given street

There are people looking for a window cleaner.

Our job in that business is to find those people.

Today is not the right day for 95% of the people we talk to.

So we'll come by again in a few months.

We want to be top of mind when the time is right for them.

Show a lifeguard a drowning man, she leaps into action.

Call to Action is how you inspire people to stay in touch.

So how do you stay top of mind?

Offer something of value in exchange for people's contact information.

There are two reasons for this.

First, sending them something gives you an excuse to follow up with them. It's much more memorable to send someone something they asked for than just to send a generic "It was nice meeting you yesterday" email.

Second, they will look forward to hearing from you. You're not an annoyance or bother. You're sending them something they asked for.

It's a great way to start a relationship.

It's a great reason to follow up after an event.

Here are five things you can do to inspire your prospects to action.

1. Invite them to join your email newsletter list

"Just hand me your card with the word 'Tips' on it and I'll send you my monthly (Elevator Pitch, Home Improvement, Leadership, Hurricane Preparedness) Tips Email Newsletter"

2. Offer them a "7 Biggest Mistakes" White Paper

"If you're interested in our free white paper on the 7 Biggest Mistakes people make when (buying a home, investing their money, business networking, …) just hand me your card and I'll be happy to send it to you."

3. Schedule a complimentary 20 minute phone consultation

"If you're interested in more ways to (make your backyard more inviting, set up an effective interview process, run payroll more efficiently) just come up to me afterwards and we can schedule a 20-minute complimentary phone call."

4. Invite them to a free webinar

"If you're interested in attending our free webinar for (technology startups, real-estate professionals, general contractors) just hand me your card and I'll send you more information."

5. Mention a job opening at your company

"We're growing really fast and need a top-notch (office manager, Java developer, racecar driver) so if you know of anyone looking for that kind of job, please hand me your business card and we appreciate the referral."

Notice that in all of these cases you ask for a business card. You do not just want to hand out information (i.e. your white paper) because then you have no way to follow up with people.

Go ahead and pull out the worksheet at the end of the book, and fill out a Call to Action for your business.

So, we've talked about grabbing their attention with a power question.

Starting the conversation with a client success story.

And calling them to action to collect their contact information.

When you put these all together on the same page in your worksheet, that gives you a fully formed Elevator Pitch.

Here are some examples to look at as you develop your Elevator Pitch:

"Do you have a pre-nuptial agreement for your business? I recently had to dissolve a business partnership. I really wish they would have come to me when they were setting up the partnership, because I could have clarified the relationship and drastically increased their chances of survival. If you want to know the 7 biggest mistakes people make when setting up a business partnership, just hand me your card and I'll be happy to send you a copy of our free white paper."

"Have you ever been at a birthday party where you had as much fun as the kids? One parent recently went to my website and booked a party for her son that featured the balloon pop race. One kid sat so hard on his balloon that it sailed behind his back, and the parents were laughing just as hard as the kids. If you're interested in delighting your kid at their next birthday party, just come up and let me know your kid's birthday so we can reserve the date."

"When was the last time you looked at your insurance coverage pages? I was working with someone who owned several restaurant locations. He faxed over his insurance pages and I quickly discovered that he did not have liquor liability coverage at one of his locations that served alcohol. What gaps do you think might be hiding in your insurance coverage?"

You can find more examples plus additional Elevator Pitch resources at http://improvandy.com/examples

Congratulations!

You've reached the end, which is really the beginning.

You know that details start conversations.

You know the difference between a Conversational and a 30-Second Elevator Pitch.

You've developed engaging answers to the only three questions you'll ever be asked at any networking event.

You've created an authentic, personalized power question, client success story, and call to action, and tied them together into an effective 30-Second Elevator Pitch.

And that's just the first skill!

Business networking success starts with the Elevator Pitch, gains momentum with effective follow up and 1-on-1's, then hits its stride with professional referrals and opportunity spotting.

That's when you become a Trusted Advisor, the go-to person who has a Rolodex of quality people.

The Elevator Pitch is the first of the Five Skills of the Trusted Advisor.

Visit our online course catalog to learn more.

http://courses.improvandy.com

I want you to grow your business more rapidly using less energy, time, and effort.

A great lead for me is a business association or networking group that brings in keynote speakers. Feel free to reach out to me to sign up for my coaching programs or to invite me to speak to your organization.

Your partner in continued success,

Andrew Winig
Elevator Pitch Coach and Keynote Speaker

IMPROV**ANDY**™
improving team performance

WHAT DO YOU DO?

Answers to the only 3 questions
you'll ever be asked at any networking event

1. "How's it going?"

_____:
{Awesome!}

I just _____.
{something awesome you just did}

2. "What do you do?"

I help _____
{a group of people}

_____.
{take an action}

3. "How do you do that?"

A _____ approached
{business}

me through _____
{referral}

because _____.
{reason}

I'm very happy to report that we have rolled out our

_____ which
{project}

addresses their _____ and
{challenge}

gives them _____.
{benefit}

ELEVATOR PITCH CPR
The 30-Second Elevator Pitch Worksheet

THE ABC's of CPR   Elevator Pitch CPR

AIRWAY   A   _____

BREATHING   B   _____

CIRCULATION   C   _____

POWER QUESTION

When was the last time _____?

Everyone knows that _____. You may

be doing _____.

I work with people who are _____.

CLIENT SUCCESS

Think about a particular customer you work with who is a perfect customer:

> √ Their issues are right in your wheelhouse
> √ They are delighted with your work
> √ You want more customers like them

How did this customer find you?

_____

Why were they looking for you?

_____

What business are they in?

_____

What were (are) their challenges?

_____

How do you help them?

_____

What benefits do they see?

_____

CLIENT SUCCESS

I was approached by a _____ who
{type of business}

was facing _____.
{business challenge}

We rolled out our _____ and
{product or service}

now they _____.
{benefit}

CALL TO ACTION

Free copy of the 7 Biggest Mistakes People Make When

They _____.

When you're ready to take control of your

_____.

A great referral for me is a _____

_____.

POWER QUESTION

I'm going to tell you about a recent client success...

CLIENT SUCCESS

I was approached by a _____ who
{type of business}

was facing _____.
{business challenge}

We rolled out our _____ and
{product or service}

now they _____.
{benefit}

CALL TO ACTION

My name is _____ and
{your name}

if you want to avoid the **7 Biggest Mistakes** people make

when they _____ then
{business activity}

hand me your business card and I'll email you our free

White Paper.

NEXT STEPS

ELEVATOR PITCH TIPS EMAIL NEWSLETTER:
ElevatorPitchTips.com

3-WEEK ELEVATOR PITCH HOME STUDY COURSE:
ElevatorPitchAtHome.com

TRUSTED ADVISOR COMMUNITY WEBINAR SERIES:
TrustedAdvisorCommunity.com